Koalas

Victoria Blakemore

vblakemore.author@gmail.com

Copyright info/picture credits

Cover, Renate Micallef/AdobeStock; Page 3, saskia1310/ Pixabay; Page 5, wisannumkarng/AdobeStock; Page 7, Successful4/Pixabay; Page 9, Mingman Srilakorn/AdobeStock; Pages 10-11, mwhaskin/AdobeStock; Page 13, Dominik Rueß/ AdobeStock; Page 15, Pexels/Pixabay; Page 17, Greg Brave/ Adobestock; Page 19, Pexels/Pixabay; Page 21, Pexels/ Pixabay; Page 23; Renate Micallef/AdobeStock; Page 25, LoneWolfAlphaCoders/Pixabay; Page 27, talk2vic/Pixabay; Page 29, RuRu_SG/Pixabay; Page 31, filipefrazao/AdobeStock; Page 33, Rafael Ben-Ari/AdobeStock

Table of Contents

What Are Koalas?

Koalas are a special kind of mammal called a **marsupial**. This means that they have a pouch on their stomach.

They are known for their fluffy ears and spoon-shaped nose.

Size

Koalas grow to be almost three feet long and can weigh up to 35 pounds.

Male koalas are usually longer and heavier than female koalas.

Koalas have a small brain
for an animal of their size.
This may be because it
doesn't need much energy.

Physical Characteristics

Koalas can be silver gray or chocolate brown. They have extra fur on their bottom. It works as padding for sitting on hard tree branches.

They also have a curved backbone. It lets them fit easily between tree branches.

Koalas have sharp claws that

they use for climbing.

Habitat

Koalas are found in eucalyptus forests. The trees provide koalas shelter, food, and protection from **predators** such as dingoes.

They are rarely seen on the ground.

Koalas spend most of their time in trees, sleeping and eating.

Range

Koalas are only found in the eastern parts of Australia.

Most koalas are found in the New South Wales and Queensland states of Australia.

Diet

Koalas are **herbivores**. They usually eat leaves from the eucalyptus tree. They can eat up to 2.5 pounds of leaves each day.

Koalas also sometimes eat other leaves, flowers, and fruit.

Eucalyptus leaves have a lot of water in them, so koalas don't need to drink very often.

Eucalyptus leaves have very little **protein**. They do not provide much energy.

Eucalyptus leaves also have **toxins** that make them poisonous to most animals. Koalas are one of the few mammals that can eat them.

Koalas spend up to 20

hours each day sleeping

in the trees.

Communication

Koalas use sound to communicate with other koalas. They make a loud, bellowing call to let other koalas know where they are.

Mother koalas also use clicking and squeaking noises with their babies.

Koalas also use scent to mark their territory. It lets other koalas know the area is taken.

Movement

Koalas have two **opposable digits** on their front paws. They are able to use their front paws to grip tree branches for climbing.

Koalas do not have a tail, but they have very good balance.

Koalas spend most of their time

in trees, but sometimes climb

down to the ground.

Koala Joeys

Koalas usually have one baby, which is called a joey. When they are first born, joeys are about the size of a jellybean.

Joeys stay in their mother's pouch for between six and seven months.

Once they are old enough, joeys

can begin to climb trees and

feed themselves.

Senses

Koalas have a very good sense of smell. They use it to smell eucalyptus leaves to see how many toxins are in the leaves.

Koalas are very picky about what they eat. They won't eat leaves that have too many toxins.

Koalas also have a very good

sense of hearing. Their eyesight

is not very good.

Solitary Life

Koalas are not very social animals, and spend most of their time alone. Females are more social than males.

Male koalas are usually **territorial**. They mark their territory with special scent glands.

Koalas spend most of their time alone, sleeping in the trees.

Koala Bears?

Koalas are often called "koala bears," but they are not really bears.

They look similar to bears, which is why people started calling them that.

Koalas are actually more

closely related to the wombat,

another Australian marsupial.

Population

Koalas are not **endangered**, but there are fewer koalas now than there used to be.

Habitat loss and predators are the biggest problem facing koalas.

Studies show that there may be

fewer than 80,000 koalas left in

the wild.

Helping Koalas

Eucalyptus forests are being cut down to make spaces for buildings and roads. This is a big problem for koalas, who need a lot of space.

Koala populations have been **declining** due to the habitat loss.

The Australian Koala Foundation is a group that works to help koalas.

They focus on **conserving** koala habitats, researching koalas, and tracking koala population.

Koalas in the wild usually live

between twelve and

eighteen years.

Glossary

Conserving: keeping safe

Declining: getting smaller

Endangered: at risk of becoming extinct

Herbivore: an animal that eats only plants

Marsupial: a special kind of mammal that has a pouch

Opposable digit: a finger that is able to grasp objects

Predator: an animal that hunts and eats other animals

Protein: a source of energy found in food

Territorial: when an animal is very protective of an area

Toxins: a poisonous substance

About the Author

Victoria Blakemore is a first grade teacher in Southwest Florida with a passion for reading.

You can visit her at www.elementaryexplorers.com

Also in This Series

Also in This Series